West Virginia
The Land and its People

West Virginia

Contents

Introduction   7
West Virginia Facts   10
Geology   14
Prehistory   22
Blennerhassett Island   28
Civil War   34
Coal Mining   44
Railroads   52
New River Gorge National River   58
Monongahela National Forest   68
State Parks and Forests   80
Capitol Complex   94
Tamarack   100
National Radio Astronomy Observatory   106
The People of West Virginia   120
Acknowledgments   128

Second Edition - 2003
International Standard Book Number
    ISBN 0-9623153-6-2
Library of Congress Catalogue Card Number
    99-72702
Copyright, Photographs Arnout Hyde Jr. 1999
            Text Lucia K. Hyde 1999
    All rights reserved
Graphic Design, D Design, Denise Dodson
Printed in China, Everbest Printing, Ltd.
Published by Cannon Graphics, Inc.
                Charleston, West Virginia
No portion of this book, either photographs or
text, may be reproduced in any form without
the permission of Cannon Graphics, Inc.

Cover - Seneca Rocks, a 900-foot-tall strata of Tuscarora sandstone, adorns the South Branch Valley in the Monongahela National Forest.

Preceeding Pages - Teasels on a misty morning in Randolph and Pendleton counties

The Tygart Valley River forms a swift falls at Valley Falls State Park, south of Fairmont.

Introduction

Photographer Arnout Hyde Jr. and I present the following book as a tribute to the strength, beauty and history of West Virginia's land and people. Once a remote wilderness inhabited by a succession of Native American cultures, the land now called West Virginia witnessed the arrival of German and Scotch-Irish settlers in the 1700s. The rise of industry from natural resources and the construction of railroads followed in the next century. The blood of the Civil War fell on West Virginia soil and secured its statehood. Soon after, Italian and eastern European immigrants, as well as African-Americans, moved to the hills and hollows of the new state as stone masons, miners and lumberjacks. West Virginia's history overflows with stories of hardship and triumph, but above all it remains the history of a proud and unbreakable people in a rich and rugged land.

Today, coal, gas and other natural resources continue to fuel West Virginia's economy, although a new industry—tourism—has begun to capitalize on the state's remaining wilderness and strong arts and crafts tradition. The development of the West Virginia State Park system in the late 1920s raised awareness and access to the state's multiplicity of recreational opportunities and historical sites. West Virginia's scenic beauty and varied terrain now hold international renown among outdoor enthusiasts. Whitewater rafting and kayaking, skiing, rock climbing, hunting, fishing, backpacking and mountain biking have become some

While resting "just a spell," one mountaineer takes in the majesty of her mountain home.

of the Mountain State's more popular outdoor activities, as well as mainstays of the tourism trade. Built to showcase the work of West Virginia's artisans, the Tamarack center also draws tourists interested in the state's vivid cultural heritage.

I appreciate the honor of collaborating with my father, Arnout Hyde Jr., in publishing *West Virginia: The Land and its People*, as I respect and love him as both an artist and a parent. We have selected 13 subjects through which to present some of West Virginia's history, beauty and modern points of interest. Arranged chronologically, the subjects start with the state's geologic formation and work up to the radio astronomy research presently conducted at the National Radio Astronomy Observatory, Green Bank. The last chapter we saved for celebrating West Virginia's most valuable resource—its people. Choosing which parts of the Mountain State's land and people to highlight proved exceptionally difficult, as the state offers an abundance of possible topics.

As you read and view *West Virginia: The Land and its People*, my father and I hope that the book will bring you some measure of appreciation for our magnificent state, West Virginia.

Lucia K. Hyde

Left - Constructed of parts salvaged from old mills across the state, Glade Creek Grist Mill in Babcock State Park offers visitors freshly-ground cornmeal and buckwheat flour.

Left - Snowshoe Resort's Cupp Run, set against a backdrop of snow-dusted hills, exemplifies West Virginia's wealth of recreational opportunities and scenic beauty.

Below - Ice-encrusted branches lend the delicate appearance of crystal to trees in Pendleton County.

West Virginia Facts

State Motto:	*Montani Semper Liberi* - Mountaineers Are Always Free	
Location:	In the Appalachian region, bordering Virginia, Maryland, Pennsylvania, Ohio and Kentucky	
Area:	24,231 square miles, including 294 miles of commercially navigable waterways 41st in size among the states	
Elevation:	*Highest Point:*	Spruce Knob (Pendleton County) 4,863 feet above sea level
	Lowest Point:	Harpers Ferry (Jefferson County) 247 feet above sea level
Population:	*1990 Census:*	1,793,477
	1998 Estimate:	1,811,156
Government:	*Congress:*	Two U.S. senators; Four U.S. representatives
	Electoral Votes:	Six
	State Legislature:	34 senators; 100 delegates
	Counties:	55
Capital:	Charleston	
Statehood:	June 20, 1863; the 35th state	
State Bird:	Cardinal	
State Flower:	Rhododendron	
State Tree:	Sugar Maple	
State Animal:	Black Bear	
Primary Industries:	*Agriculture:*	Milk, eggs, apples, cattle, poultry
	Manufacturing:	Chemicals, primary metals, fabricated metal products, stone, clay and glass products, nonelectric machinery
	Mining:	Coal, petroleum, natural gas, natural gas liquids, sand and gravel
National Forests:	Monongahela, Jefferson and George Washington totaling one million acres	
State Parks:	37 totaling 74,813 acres	
State Forests:	9 totaling 78,982 acres	

Honey in the Rock

In celebration of West Virginia Day, fireworks erupt at the conclusion of the June 20th performance of *Honey in the Rock*. The outdoor drama portrays the story of West Virginia's tumultuous journey to statehood.

With the hay harvested, the serenity of late summer settles over a farm near Bartow.

A field of summer flowers and towering clouds at Canaan Valley State Park

Geology

Text by Amy Whitaker

West Virginia's landscape has undergone sweeping changes throughout geologic history. Only traces of the ancient seas, swamps and great mountains that once comprised the area now called West Virginia remain in rocks and landforms throughout the state.

West Virginia contains mostly sedimentary rocks including sandstone, limestone, shale and coal. The rocks formed from the deposition of loose particles that became buried under successive layers of sediment. Eventually the weight of overlaying material compacted the particles into rock. In many cases, the rocks subsequently folded deep within the earth. Many millennia of erosion erased the thousands of feet of overlaying soil and sediment to expose the rocks visible today.

During the early part of West Virginia's geologic history, from approximately 550 to 350 million years ago, the state lay at the bottom of a shallow ocean west of a pre-North American continent. The thick layers of limestone deposited during this age still contain fossilized sea shells.

In geology's Pennsylvanian Epoch, 340 to 280 million years ago, as sea levels fluctuated, West Virginia became alternately a warm shallow sea and a humid coastal plain. The swamps of Pennsylvanian-age West Virginia created the state's many coal seams. Subject to long periods of intense heat and pressure, collections of decaying organic swamp matter metamorphosed into the rich bituminous coal known today as "black gold" in the West Virginia coal fields.

Some 250 million years ago, present-day Africa collided with North America, lifting the Appalachian Mountains higher than today's Himalayas. This mountain building event compressed some of West Virginia's rock layers into a series of ridge tops and valley bottoms. Inclined strata in the eastern part of the state, such as Seneca Rocks in Pendleton County, reflect the folding episode. Seneca Rocks represents one of the remaining pieces of the vertical limb of an ancient fold.

The appearance of West Virginia's modern landscape results predominately from erosion. Rivers have carved narrow valleys. In some cases ancient mountain tops wore down farther than the valleys. Therefore, prehistoric basins and valleys now constitute many of West Virginia's highest points. Some still act as water collectors, creating the state's modern high elevation wetlands.

In eastern West Virginia, due to high concentrations of limestone, solution weathering creates caverns and sinkholes. The calcium carbonate in the limestone dissolves as groundwater passes through it, causing the development of caves and springs. When the sedimentary strata overlaying a cave roof becomes too heavy for the roof to support, the ceiling of the cave collapses, forming a bowl-shaped depression called a sinkhole.

West Virginia's terrain, with rugged hills and wild rivers, has long influenced the state's history, economy and people. From the struggles of early settlers to traverse the mountains, to coal mining, to whitewater rafting and rock climbing, the people of West Virginia have found challenge, sustenance and prosperity in the land.

Distant hills echo the stillness of Droop Mountain Battlefield in Pocahontas County.

Bear Rocks in Dolly Sods

Boulders in the Monongahela National Forest

The Potomac River at Harpers Ferry

*W*ind and water
continue to
sculpt the face
of West Virginia.

Opposite Page - One of the many rock outcroppings along the Blackwater Canyon in Tucker County.

Left - Giant spires of Tuscarora sandstone from the Silurian Age form Judy Rocks in Pendleton County.

Through the ages, wind, snow and ice have eroded a large formation of Droop sandstone on the summit of Droop Mountain in Beartown State Park, Pocahontas and Greenbrier counties. Extensive boardwalks allow guests to view the rocks without disturbing the delicate ecology thriving on their surfaces.

Above - Lost World Caverns, near
Lewisburg, feature a chamber 1,000-feet
long and up to 75-feet wide that ranks as
one of the most voluminous subterranean
rooms known in the world today.

Left - An aerial view of the South Branch
of the Potomac River shows the winding
course the river has carved through the
Smoke Hole Region.

Prehistory

Before the first European settlers traversed the area now called West Virginia in the 1700s, a succession of distinct Native American cultures had already occupied the land for approximately 14,000 years.

As early as 13,000 BCE, small nomadic groups roamed the mid-North American continent, tracking large game herds such as mastodons, woolly mammoths and bison. Known today as the Paleo-Indian people, the early hunters used fluted projectile points, spearheads with a vertical groove, to fell their prey. Archaeologists have discovered the ancient points scattered throughout West Virginia, with the highest concentration near Parkersburg, Wood County.

The gradual extinction of many prehistoric mammals between 7000 and 6000 BCE created a food shortage for the Paleo-Indian people and gave rise to a new "gathering" based culture labeled the Archaic Foragers. By supplementing their collection of seeds, nuts, roots, berries and freshwater shell fish with small game hunting, the Archaic Foragers enjoyed a fairly stable diet that led to an increase in population and more time for ceremonial activities.

The St. Albans site in Kanawha County shows evidence of seasonal habitation dating to 7000 BCE. Transitory gatherers most likely camped on the spot while harvesting mussels from the nearby Kanawha River. Both the northern panhandle and the eastern counties of West Virginia also contain artifacts, including bone tools, flint and stone blades, and hide scrappers that indicate the presence of the Archaic Foragers.

In the latter portion of the Archaic Period, the Transitional Archaic (2000 -1000 BCE), bands of foragers began cultivating sunflower seeds, pigweed and goosefoot, fashioning vessels from stone and producing a crude form of pottery. Archaeologists also have noted the appearance of grave goods and ceremonial red pigment in burials.

The succeeding Early Adena culture's mastery of horticulture practices allowed the Adena to establish settlements. Residing primarily in the Ohio Valley, the Early Adena built wood and bark round houses and simple burial mounds.

In roughly 500 BCE, Adena society began to reflect influences of the Hopewell people, another Native American group inhabiting the southern portion of the Ohio Valley. During the ensuing half-century referred to as the Late Adena Period, the Adena, like the Hopewell, constructed large burial mounds with intricate tombs especially for shamen. Graves included substantial goods such as copper jewelry. Pottery quality improved and the Adena picked up the Hopewell art of carving animal figurines, pendants and pipes.

Many archaeologists believe that the Adena and Hopewell societies eventually intermixed in the Kanawha Valley, forming the Armstrong Culture. The Armstrong invented a unique form of delicate, yellow-orange pottery, and also began using cremation in addition to burial mounds. The Armstrong people may have evolved into the Buck Garden Culture that inhabited central West Virginia from approximately CE 500 to CE 1200. The first to grow corn, beans and squash, the Buck Garden society lived in compact villages and used natural rock overhangs as grave sites. Warfare with other Native American cultures most likely dispersed the Buck Garden people into the surrounding hills.

Chronologically parallel to the Armstrong and Buck Garden cultures, the Wilhelm Stone Cist Mound Builders and then the Watson Farm Stone Mound Builders thrived in the northern panhandle. As their names indicate, they constructed burial mounds predominately of rock.

During the Late Prehistoric Period (CE 1000 - CE 1700) two main Native American groups, the Fort Ancient People in the Kanawha and Ohio valleys and the Monongahela Culture in the north, populated West Virginia. Although both groups built oval or circular stockaded villages and practiced home burials, the Fort Ancients dwelt in rectangular houses, while the Monongahela constructed dome shelters. Ceramic bowls and jars, human and animal shaped figurines and mussel shell jewelry represent some of the many artifacts belonging to the Late Prehistoric Period.

Eventually, European trade goods such as brass kettles, iron tools and glass objects appear among indigenous artifacts at village sites. However, only 50 years following initial contact with Europeans, most Native American societies abandoned their settlements in West Virginia. Archaeologists blame exposure to new diseases and aggression from northern Iroquois tribes for the depopulation. West Virginia, henceforth, served as a hunting ground and thoroughfare for bands of Mingo, Shawnee, Delaware, Seneca, Canoy and Tuscarora Indians.

A petroglyph (rock carving) in Wyoming County, near Oceana

Shadows haunt the Adena burial mound in South Charleston.

*V*estiges of West Virginia's prehistoric past remain in the form of burial mounds, rock carvings and artifacts.

Following pages - Clouds shroud the New River Valley between the West Virginia and Virginia border at Narrows, Virginia.

Cathedral State Park, a 133-acre
forest in Preston County, constitutes
one of the few stands of virgin
timber left in the state. The park
preserves the appearance of West
Virginia's woodland areas before
the advent of industrial logging.

Blennerhassett Island

Just south of Parkersburg, the waters of the Ohio River part around the shores of "Paradise." With majestic sycamore trees and remote serenity, Blennerhassett Island once gained the nicknames "Paradise" and "Eden." Now preserved as a West Virginia historical state park, the island boasts a history as rich and colorful as its scenic beauty.

Archaeological excavations on Blennerhassett Island have uncovered evidence of human habitation as early as the Paleo-Indian period (10,000 - 8000 BCE). During the Woodland Indian period (CE 1000 - CE 1700) at least three Native American villages thrived on the island.

During the Indian War of 1791-1795, terrorized residents of Belpre in the Northwest Territory (now Ohio) built two blockhouses on the island, naming their haven Belpre Island.

The island's most famous residents, Harman and Margaret Blennerhassett, purchased their piece of fleeting paradise from the island's Connecticut owner, Elijah Backus, in 1799. Wealthy aristocrats, the newly wed Harman and niece Margaret had sailed to the United States to escape political turmoil and marital scandal in Ireland.

Construction of the Blennerhassett mansion began with the clearing of a stand of sycamore trees from one of the island's highest points. When completed, the central structure rose two and a half stories and contained 12 rooms. Graceful porticos arched from the front corners of the mansion to connect a dependency building on each side. One wing housed the kitchen, while the other served as Harman's study. The interior boasted black walnut paneling, oriental rugs, small sculptures, fine paintings, alabaster lamps and other treasures the couple had imported from Europe, Philadelphia and Baltimore.

The Blennerhassetts supervised the cultivation of a 2 1/3 acre garden flowering with local and exotic plants, including hothouses of citrus fruit trees. The estate also supported 100 cleared acres of crops, barns, and stables.

The Blennerhassetts hosted numerous cultural events that drew a succession of famous guests to their palace in the wilderness, including Charles X of France and Johnny Appleseed. One such visitor would destroy their paradise. Former vice-president of the United States Aaron Burr persuaded the Blennerhassetts to let him use their island as the headquarters for his expedition to invade Mexico and establish a new nation.

Burr's co-conspirator, Brigadier-General James Wilkinson, betrayed Burr's schemes to President Jefferson. The local Virginia militia raided the island in December 1806. Harman and Burr escaped downriver, but failed to elude capture. Both charged with high treason, Burr's acquittal also exonerated Harman. During the island invasion, Margaret and her two sons fled, eventually reuniting with Harman to operate an unsuccessful plantation in the Mississippi Territory.

Shortly after the Blennerhassetts' flight, the Neale family of Virginia moved into the Blennerhassett mansion. On March 3, 1811, they awoke to flames that consumed the house. The Neales managed to escape the blaze, but the fire's origin remains a mystery.

Beyond the gutted mansion, George Neale Jr. constructed a brick house in 1833. After 1840, Colonel John M. Johnson resided in the home, where he hosted the famous poet Walt Whitman. Whitman wrote a poem on the splendor of Blennerhassett Island hailing it "Queen of the Waters."

On May 1,1886, Amos W. Gordon opened a public leisure park at the island's head. Up to 15,000 people each summer flocked to Gordon's dance pavilion, picnic tables, bowling alley, boxing ring and baseball diamond. Here, the U.S. Heavyweight boxing champion (1892 - 1897) "Gentleman Jim" Corbett staged an exhibition match, and such famous baseball teams as the Cincinnati Reds, the Pittsburgh Pirates and the Brooklyn Dodgers challenged local players. However, the "Great Flood of 1913" wiped out the island enterprise. The E. I. DuPont de Nemours and Company later purchased the island, closing the land to public use.

In 1972 the West Virginia legislature created a legislative agency called the "Blennerhassett Historical Commission." The state of West Virginia leased the upper portion of the island from DuPont to open Blennerhassett Historical State Park on July 27, 1980. Work began in 1984 to rebuild the Blennerhassett mansion.

Today, Blennerhassett Historical State Park offers tours of the mansion's furnished interior and special events such as "The Mansion by Candlelight" and "Christmas on the Island." Horse-drawn wagon rides and walking paths enable visitors to explore the upper half of the island, while the Blennerhassett Museum in downtown Parkersburg offers a unique look into the extensive history of Blennerhassett Island.

Bikers ride past the Blennerhassett mansion.

The old carriage road leads visitors into Blennerhassett Island's intriguing past.

A team of Percheron draft horses draw passengers on wagon rides around the upper half of the island.

*P*rehistoric villages, a frontier palace and a former leisure park all figure into the colorful history of Blennerhassett Island.

Following pages -
An aerial view of
Blennerhassett
Island at dusk

Above - Horses grazing in pastures along the Ohio River.

Right - Black-eyed-susans cluster around an old fence post near the Ohio River.

The Civil War and Statehood

Born of the Civil War, the area now called West Virginia played an integral part in the bitter conflict that divided the nation. During the initial hostilities in 1861, Union and Confederate forces struggled for control of western Virginia as the region formed the frontier between north and south and included such important transportation routes as the Kanawha Turnpike and the Baltimore and Ohio Railroad.

Even before the first shots of the Civil War the growing turmoil over the issue of slavery erupted on western Virginia soil. On October 16, 1859 slavery abolitionist John Brown raided the Federal arsenal at Harpers Ferry in hopes of capturing the town and instigating a slave revolt in the south. Arrested, tried and hanged for treason, Brown became a hero for the anti-slavery movement of the north.

Four days after the outbreak of war at Fort Sumpter on April 13, 1861, the state of Virginia passed an ordinance of secession from the Federal government despite the disapproval of its 34 western counties. Delegates from the western region met at two Wheeling Conventions to establish the "Restored Government of Virginia" and to debate the formation of a new state loyal to the Union.

Following Virginia's secession, Colonel Thomas "Stonewall" Jackson seized Harpers Ferry for the south. The B & O Railroad, which provided the only continuous route from Baltimore to the Ohio River, passed through Harpers Ferry, making the city a strategic point for controlling one of the Union's most valuable supply lines. However, deeming Harpers Ferry indefensible from the surrounding U.S. territory, Jackson retreated on June 14, 1861.

The first Union casualty of the Civil War, Private Thornsberry Bailey Brown, as well as the war's first land battle fell, within western Virginia. While attempting to spy on an encampment of Confederate forces in Taylor County on May 22, 1861, Brown received several fatal bayonet wounds to the chest. Shortly after, on June 3rd, Federal Colonel Benjamin F. Kelley routed Confederate troops from Philippi, Barbour County. The southern forces under Colonel George Porterfield had retired to Philippi following a failed attempt to capture the B & O Railroad near Grafton. Surprised by the Union raid, the Confederates fled so quickly that the battle earned the nickname the "Philippi Races."

Several subsequent battles and numerous skirmishes carried the blood of war throughout western Virginia, including, in 1861, the battles of Rich Mountain, Scary Creek, and Carnifex Ferry, and a massive Confederate attack on Harpers Ferry that left 50 Union soldiers dead, 173 wounded and the city razed. The next year brought the Battle of Lewisburg and, in 1863, troops waged the battles of Bulltown and Droop Mountain, as well as the Battle of Winfield in 1864. Gauley Bridge, Charles Town, White Sulphur Springs and many other areas suffered smaller conflicts, raids and burnings. Some towns changed possession numerous times during the war, with Romney in Hampshire County, holding the state record of 56 exchanges.

While war raged through the western counties in the winter of 1862, the "Restored Government of Virginia" drafted a constitution for a new state. An overwhelming majority of citizens ratified the document on April 3, 1862. A year later, President Lincoln released a proclamation that on June 20, 1863, made West Virginia the 35th state admitted to the Union. In addition to the original 34 western counties, the new state included the counties of the eastern panhandle, as well as Pocahontas, Greenbrier, Monroe, Mercer and McDowell counties, despite their Confederate leanings.

While Confederate General Robert E. Lee's surrender at Appomattox, Virginia on April 9, 1865 marked the end of the Civil War, West Virginia remained a state of divided sympathies with veterans of both armies residing within the borders. A National Cemetery established in 1868 at Grafton, Taylor County, serves as the final resting place for Union and Confederate soldiers alike.

Monuments, museums and protected battle sites throughout the state commemorate the Civil War's importance in West Virginia's history. The Harpers Ferry National Historical Park, Droop Mountain State Park and Carnifex Ferry State Park all preserve former battlefields. Several groups of Civil War buffs bring to life the conflict with staged re-enactments, while Theater West Virginia's long-running outdoor drama, *Honey in the Rock*, portrays the state's formation from the struggles of war.

A Union soldier caps his musket.

"Charge!" The 11th Virginia cavalry thundering into battle.

A Union family pauses for a final portrait before battle.

Civil War minister Jason Bauserman and wife in reflection at Travellers Repose

Remembering the battles of Rich Mountain and Travellers Repose

Left - The Philippi Covered Bridge, originally built in 1852 and rebuilt after a fire in 1991, crosses the Tygart Valley River. Philippi marks the site of the first land battle of the Civil War.

Below - The 1st West Virginia Light Artillery A unleashes a cannon blast at Travellers Repose, near Bartow.

Gas lights line the streets of Harpers Ferry in Jefferson County, adding an antiquated atmosphere to a town steeped in Civil War history. The slavery abolitionist John Brown made his famous arsenal raid here in 1859.

The cemetery at St. James' Lutheran Church south of Shepherdstown remains the final resting place of several Civil War soldiers including William Hendricks, a member of the Stonewall Brigade in the first battle of Manassas. The founding of St. James' Lutheran church dates to 1765.

Organ Cave, near Ronceverte, provided saltpetre (potassium nitrate) for making black powder during the Civil War. Thirty-seven of the 52 original saltpetre hoppers used to leach the mineral salt from cave soil remain in the cave. One of the longest caves in the United States, Organ Cave has more than 40-miles of mapped passageways.

Following pages - Harpers Ferry viewed from Maryland Heights on a misty summer morning.

Coal Mining

Beneath West Virginia's rugged beauty lie vast seams of bituminous coal that have shaped both the state's history and the nation's economy since the 1800s. An estimated 117 billion tons of mineable coal once ran through the mountains' depths, with approximately 100 billion tons remaining today. Out of all 55 West Virginia counties, only Jefferson and Hardy counties do not contain coal deposits.

Despite John Peter Salley's discovery of coal in what is now West Virginia in 1742, the resource did not gain commercial importance until 1817, when salt works in the Kanawha Valley began using coal to heat salt brine. Small mines in the eastern panhandle supplied coal to the Federal arsenal at Harpers Ferry, while the construction of the Baltimore and Ohio Railroad in the early 1850s allowed the northern coal fields to serve Baltimore and other eastern cities. The 1873 completion of the Chesapeake and Ohio Railroad provided access to extensive coal deposits in the New River and Kanawha valleys. However, not until the Norfolk and Western Railway opened in the mid 1880s could coal companies capitalize on the immense resource wealth of southern West Virginia.

Early mining techniques relied solely on human and animal labor to recover and haul coal from within the earth. Often, children worked in the mines separating shale from coal, opening ventilation doors and stopping escaped coal carts. By the 1920s, electric locomotives replaced animals used to transport coal to the surface and child labor laws forbade youth employment. The following decade, coal-cutting machines such as the continuous miner began the evolution of coal mining into a highly mechanized industry.

The coal industry's rapid development in the late 1800s drew a huge labor force of primarily European immigrants and African-Americans to West Virginia. Coal companies built entire towns, including primitive housing for miners and their families. Due to the remote location of many mining towns, the companies also operated supply stores stocked with essential goods from clothing to groceries. Many mining towns formed their own baseball team, choir and theater guild.

The poverty, overcrowding and unsanitary conditions that characterized life in numerous coal camps led to disease outbreaks, while mine accidents, such as roof falls and explosions, claimed additional lives. Some coal companies also practiced a slew of abuses that added to the hardships of miners and their families. Company weighmen knew tricks to slight wages and many companies further controlled workers by paying them in scrip. Often miners could only use the scrip to "purchase" overpriced provisions at the company store. Requiring miners to live in company-owned houses also gave mine owners power over their employees.

While many early miners struggled with destitution, owners of large mining companies, known as "coal barons," grew rich from exporting millions of tons of coal and a by-product, coke, to destinations throughout the United States. Coal mined from southern West Virginia fueled construction of the Panama Canal in the early 1900s, while the nation depended on West Virginia coal to operate factories 24-hours a day during World Wars I and II.

Coal company injustices against miners and the disparity of wealth between employers and employees culminated in a long and bloody struggle to unionize the coal fields. Beginning with a massive miners' strike on Paint Creek and Cabin Creek in Kanawha County, in 1912, the turmoil continued for 21 years until the National Industrial Recovery Act established the right of workers to join labor unions.

To combat unionization, coal companies forced workers to sign pledges against joining the United Mine Workers of America, evicted union sympathizers from company housing and, on at least one occasion, fired machine guns at an encampment of striking miners. Several armed skirmishes erupted between miners and the Baldwin-Felts guards hired to resist union efforts. Known as the "West Virginia Mine Wars," the Mucklow Battle, the Matewan Massacre and the Battle of Blair Mountain that prompted President Harding to send 2,000 U.S. troops to subdue fighting, were among the more deadly encounters. With the eventual legalization of labor unions in 1933, more than 300,000 miners joined the United Mine Workers in one year.

Today, the Eastern Regional Coal Archives in Bluefield preserves West Virginia's coal history, while the Beckley Exhibition Coal Mine's guided tour through a restored, turn-of-the-century mine educates guests about mining and safety techniques from the late 1800s to the present. Using advanced mining technology, West Virginia currently provides half of the total U.S. coal exports.

Visitors on a "man trip" listen to a seasoned coal miner explain a miner's lunch bucket at The Beckley Exhibition Coal Mine.

Coal baron Samuel Dixon's restored early 20th-century kitchen on display in the elegant Dixon mansion at The Beckley Exhibition Coal Mine.

The company doctor's office on the second story of the Dixon mansion

*E*xperience the past in the present at The Beckley Exhibition Coal Mine.

Following pages - One of the restored 19th-century coal mine passages open to tourists in the New River Park, Beckley.

The Kaymoor tipple in the New River
Gorge loaded high quality bituminous
coal called "smokeless coal," mined from
the Sewell seam above the tipple. The
tipple now stands a skeletal reminder of
the coal mining history in the New River
Gorge National River.

Above - The first traces of dawn illuminate the Kanawha River flowing quietly through the capital city of Charleston.

Left - Steam rises from the coal-powered plant at St. Mary's, along the Ohio River.

Railroads

On a brisk October morning a plume of smoke rises from the gold and scarlet foliage of Cheat Mountain as a 90-ton Shay locomotive lumbers toward the summit. The turn-of-the-century steam engine that once hauled timber, now transports a trainload of tourists on a Cass Scenic Railroad excursion. Like most of the Mountain State's rails, the Cass line once traversed treacherous terrain to access remote natural resources. Although railroad companies initially saw western Virginia (now West Virginia) as simply a thoroughfare for connecting the eastern seaboard to the Ohio River, railroads soon revolutionized the state's industrial production.

In 1840, the Baltimore and Ohio Railroad Company laid the first track in western Virginia after overcoming objections of the Virginia General Assembly and farmers along the proposed route. Fearing trains would kill livestock and petrify women and children, legislators stalled construction of the B&O short of Harpers Ferry for four years. However, by 1842, rails reached Cumberland, Maryland via Harpers Ferry. In 1848, work began on the B&O's final 200-mile stretch through the Allegheny Mountains to the Ohio River at Wheeling. The distance spanned the most rugged topography the railroad had yet attempted. Nevertheless, the first east coast train to reach the Ohio River arrived in Wheeling on January 1, 1853.

Wishing to also access Parkersburg on the Ohio River, the B&O installed rails to the port city that departed the mainline at Grafton. Completing the Grafton-Parkersburg route in 1857, the company later established track from Elkins to Charleston, Wheeling to Kenova, and Clarksburg to Richwood, with branch lines serving smaller communities. Towns, factories and farms grew alongside the railroad, capitalizing on the new link to markets east and west.

In the late 1850s, as secessionist sentiments circulated through the nation's southern states, the Virginia General Assembly tried to bind its union-leaning western counties to the south with a railroad between Covington and the confluence of the Guyandot and Ohio rivers. Although construction began in 1861, the Civil War interrupted worked on the line until 1868, when the Chesapeake and Ohio Railway Company acquired the abandoned project. Under direction of railroad magnate Collis P. Huntington, C&O engineers routed the railroad through the New River Gorge and along the famous wagon-road, the Kanawha Turnpike. In 1871, the company assembled the town of Huntington to serve as the C&O's western terminus on the Ohio River. When crews completed the tracks on January 2, 1873, the first train steamed out of Covington carrying a barrel of water from the James River to the C&O ceremonies in Huntington. Here, railroad officials dumped the water into the Ohio River to celebrate the new east-west connection. Within months of the C&O's arrival, access to the abundant coal seams of the New River Gorge spawned an economic explosion in the once quiet canyon.

The success of industry along the B&O and C&O lines inspired the foundation of the Norfolk and Western railroad through Mercer County to the fertile Pocahontas coalfields. Finished in 1892, the Norfolk and Western became West Virginia's primary transporter of coal, as well as one of the first railroads in the nation to replace steam locomotives with electric traction engines.

By the early 1900s, rails wound throughout the Mountain State's once impenetrable wilderness, laying bare hidden reserves of coal, timber and natural gas. Hundreds of mining towns and logging camps spread out from the tracks that served as a lifeline of income and supplies. The grind and squeal of train gears and the gentle clack of steel on steel remain the song of home to many West Virginians.

While a stream of coal-filled railroad cars persists as a familiar sight in West Virginia, many of the state's branch lines sold for scrap with the close of mines and logging operations during the latter part of the 20th-century. Passenger travel on railways also waned with the advent of interstate highways and improved airlines. However, several of West Virginia's railroads now offer tourist excursions. In addition to the Cass Scenic Railroad, the Potomac Eagle in the eastern panhandle and The Mountain State Mystery Train through the New River Gorge run sightseeing trips. The Rails to Trails organization has also converted many of the state's abandoned railbeds into mountain biking adventure trails.

Nickel-plated road engine No. 765 steams through the New River Gorge.

Shay engine No. 7 crossing a 100-foot span over the Shavers Fork River.

The "Potomac Eagle" travels through the Trough, along the South Branch of the Potomac River.

West Virginia railroad excursions blend scenic routes with rail history.

Above - Heritage Station, a restored train station and Victorian-style restaurant, in the old B&O Railroad yard in Huntington.

Left - One of the few color photographs ever taken inside the Cass repair shop, the shot captures examples of early machine-age technology and architecture. Built in 1922, the shop burned 50-years later. A modern structure that houses the Cass Scenic Railroad steam engines and rolling stock now occupies the site of the original repair shop.

The Division of Natural Resources has renovated the early homes of Cass as vacation rentals.

On February 16, 1982, a fire consumed the Cass sawmill in the Cass Scenic Railroad State Park. The remains of the sawmill and other early 20th-century logging artifacts linger as shadows of the past.

The New River Gorge

Just north of Hinton, the world's second oldest river sweeps over Sandstone Falls and into a spectacular gorge of ancient rock, dense forest and abandoned mining towns. In a series of raging rapids, the New River winds 50 miles through the canyon, passing rusting coal tipples, a rock climber's paradise of sandstone cliff bands and beneath the record-breaking New River Gorge Bridge. Although few residents live in the gorge today, vestiges and legends remain of the mining boon that once filled the valley with people, prosperity and wild times. Now designated the New River Gorge National River, the area has grown into a prime outdoor recreation destination known as "The Grand Canyon of the East."

The New River rushes through the gorge in a remnant stretch of the prehistoric Teays River's 100-million year-old stream bed. As late as the 19th-century, the gorge's steep slopes and thick forests deterred extensive exploration of the area by land. However, starting in 1812, several adventurous parties did brave the river in 50-foot boats called bateaus.

The completion of the C&O Railroad on January 27, 1873, finally afforded access to the rugged heart of the New River Gorge. The railway paralleled the New River, providing the only feasible ground route in or out of the canyon.

Only months after the first train rumbled through the gorge, a blaze of industry began to consume the quality timber and thick coal seams bulging from the hillsides. Burgeoning coal and lumber barons recruited immigrant workers to harvest the region's resources, and soon coal mines, tipples, towns and lumber camps clung to the slopes of the canyon. Mile-long lines of "beehive" ovens used to smelt coke, a by-product of coal key to the manufacture of iron and steel, smoldered along the river.

By the turn-of-the-century, more than a dozen towns thrived in the gorge, supporting a mix of new millionaires and poor miners. Saloons, gambling parlors and the swanky Dunglen Hotel catered to the influx of boom money, and, along with the gorge's isolation from the rest of the nation, contributed to an air of lawlessness in some parts of the valley.

The town of Thurmond's west side gained a particular reputation as "wide open" territory. Home of the Dunglen Hotel, featuring a lavish ballroom and 24-hour casino, the establishment hosted politicians, celebrities and professional gamblers. More than 20 trains per day delivered patrons, as well as kegs, cards and courtesans.

In the early 1930s, the coal market collapse and the Great Depression bankrupted many coal companies, leaving the gorge lined with ghost towns. Although small scale mining continued in the canyon until the 1950s, few people remained.

When whitewater enthusiast John Dragan first began offering guided raft trips on the New in 1968, the gorge had become once more a remote wilderness. Along with Dragan, other raft guides, kayakers, and a small circle of rock climbers began to explore the recreational eden of the New River Gorge. However, not until the construction of the New River Gorge bridge in 1977 and the incorporation of the region into the National Park Service the following year did the gorge once again swell with people and prosperity.

Stretching 3,000-feet across the canyon, the New River Gorge Bridge remains the longest single-span arch bridge in the world. The structure completed Appalachian Corridor L Expressway, opening interstate access to the area surrounding the gorge.

In order to protect the New River Gorge's environment, history and recreational opportunities, Congress authorized the National Park Service to purchase 63,000 acres of the canyon between Hinton and Fayetteville. Named the New River Gorge National River, the National Park Service has made the area tourist-friendly with such additions as the Canyon Rim Visitor's Center and numerous hiking and mountain biking trails. The State of West Virginia recently transferred Grandview State Park, at the head of the canyon, to Federal care as part of the New River Gorge National River. Grandview's outdoor drama company, Theater West Virginia, continues to enliven summer nights with *Honey in the Rock, Hatfields and McCoys* and other musicals in the park's amphitheater.

More than 30 commercial whitewater companies now provide river adventures, while kayakers from around the globe seek the New's challenging rapids. Rock climbers also flock to the gorge's stunning crags, and both leisure and competitive riding fuel the canyon's mountain biking scene. The gorge now draws several million people per year to its natural beauty and historical mystique.

Whitewater rafters brave a rapid on the Gauley River in the New River Gorge National River.

Winter leaves a blanket of snow in the New River Gorge.

A climber scales one of the many ancient rock walls in the gorge.

The New River Gorge:
a spectacular haven of
world-class recreation

Above - Thurmond, the town with railroad tracks for a main street, lies nestled deep in the New River Gorge. During the gorge's industrial period from 1873 to the late 1930s, Thurmond bustled as the region's premiere financial and social center.

Left - The famous New River Gorge Bridge viewed from Longpoint Overlook.

Following Pages - Morning fog fills the gorge below the main overlook at Grandview.

Above - "All Forward!" Teamwork brings rafters through another exciting rapid.

Left - Sandstone Falls below Hinton on the New River.

Rafters face a wall of water on Lower Railroad rapid.

Whitewater enthusiasts in a perilous moment as their raft capsizes mid-rapid.

Monongahela National Forest

Stretching through 10 West Virginia counties in the heart of the Allegheny Mountains, the 909,000-acre Monongahela National Forest encompasses some of West Virginia's most scenic areas. Established in 1911 to safeguard the Ohio River's tributaries from such ruinous flooding as the region experienced in 1907, as well as to remedy the scars of widespread logging, the Monongahela National Forest became part of a Federal effort to protect the headwaters of the United States' major rivers.

Today, forest management combines selective timbering and the leasing of grazing land with an array of outdoor recreational opportunities that include hiking, camping, picnicking, rock climbing, spelunking, mountain biking, horseback riding, whitewater kayaking and rafting, swimming, canoeing and skiing. The National Park Service, in conjunction with the West Virginia Division of Natural Resources, regulates game habitats and stocks streams and lakes for bountiful hunting and fishing. The Highland Scenic Highway winds through 43 miles of the national forest from Richwood to U.S. Route 219 north of Marlinton, providing a stunning drive and easy access to many of the forest's sightseeing and recreation spots.

From the summit of the Mountain State's highest peak, Spruce Knob, to the rushing cascade of Hills Creek Falls, the Monongahela National Forest offers a breathtaking variety of scenic beauty and rugged backcountry. Even a unique ecosystem of Arctic Tundra plant life thrives far south of its native climate in the forest's Cranberry Glades.

The Monongahela National Forest contains five Federally designated Wilderness Areas and one National Recreation Area. The remoteness of Otter Creek, Cranberry, Laurel Fork North, Laurel Fork South and Dolly Sods meets the national definition of wilderness as "an area where the earth and its community of life are untrammeled by man, where man himself is a visitor who does not remain." Each wilderness area offers opportunities for hiking on unmarked, little-maintained trails or for offtrail navigation into the serenity of the backcountry, where wildlife abounds and where man must pass without leaving a trace. A designated Recreation Area, Spruce Knob - Seneca Rocks draws rock climbers, hikers, picnickers and other outdoor enthusiasts.

Within the mountains of the Monongahela National Forest also lie cultural enclaves like the small Swiss village Helvetia and such historical sites as Cass Scenic Railroad State Park and the Fairfax Stone.

A remote pond in the Monongahela National Forest makes a perfect place for a beaver dam.

Traces of snow remain at Cranberry Glades in the Monongahela National Forest.

Middle Falls of Hills Creek Falls during spring thaw.

A myriad of natural wonders
await in the Monongahela
National Forest.

Above - A bee among the blossoms

Right - A white-tail doe pauses before fleeing into a thicket.

Following pages - The dramatic wind-swept landscape of Dolly Sods in the Monongahela National Forest

Above - The second highest waterfalls in
the state, Hills Creek Falls is one of the
more popular scenic attractions in the
Monongahela National Forest.

Left - Skunk Cabbage, a common plant
found in the Cranberry Glades.

An autumn view from the Dolly Sods Wilderness Area in Tucker and Randolph counties. The harsh winds that sweep across the region have left many of the trees with branches on only three sides.

During fall, blueberry bushes turn a bright red in the Dolly Sods Wilderness Area. Second growth hardwood, three-sided spruce stands, bogs, streams, beaver ponds and open "sod" areas (local name for pasture lands) form this special backcountry.

Right - A boardwalk meanders though the Cranberry Glades, allowing visitors to view the area's bog vegetation, flowers, and other plant life typically native to more northern climates.

Below - Autumn turns ferns a rich brown hue in the Cranberry Glades.

State Parks and Forests

Beyond West Virginia's mineral and agricultural wealth, the people of the Mountain State have long looked to the land as a source of recreation, beauty and pride. The establishment of the West Virginia State Park system in the late 1920s began the formal preservation of some of the state's choice areas for public use. Using the criteria of scenic significance, ecological importance, historic value and recreational potential to select property, the park system has grown to protect and promote a variety of West Virginia's treasures in the form of parks, forests and wildlands.

In August 1928 the West Virginia legislature purchased the Civil War battlefield at Droop Mountain as the first piece of the state park system. Although the newly formed State Forest, Park and Conservation Commission also recommended numerous other spots for procurement, the Great Depression halted efforts to start a park system.

In the depths of the depression that plunged more than 13 million Americans into unemployment and poverty, President Franklin D. Roosevelt implemented a flurry of economic reform programs. One such program, the Civilian Conservation Corps (CCC) hired young men as public works laborers. Required to live in military-style camps, the youths received food, clothing, dental care and a monthly salary, as well as learned trade skills. The CCC also employed adept architects, engineers and other professionals. Buying land for Babcock, Lost River, Watoga, Cacapon, Hawks Nest and Grandview in 1933, the state relied on the CCC to outfit the new parks with roads, guest cabins, restaurants and other facilities.

The West Virginia State Parks struggled through the 1940s with limited resources and few visitors due to the nation's involvement in World War II. When conservationist Kermit McKeever received the appointment of Chief of the Division of State Parks in 1948, many parks lacked proper maintenance and equipment. Later nicknamed "The Father of the State Park System" for his 29 years of visionary leadership, McKeever instigated a wave of growth and improvements.

During the 1950s, in response to the country's post-war economic security and growing interest in travel, the West Virginia State Park system increased park holdings, built 89 new rental cabins, installed utilities, constructed lodges at Cacapon and Blackwater Falls, and completed the Grandview Amphitheater. The park system's first campground opened at Watoga in 1953, with 18 sites at a fee of 50 cents each per night.

In the following decade Federal grants and private and corporate land donations allowed the development of the Cass Scenic Railroad and of the resort parks Canaan Valley, Pipestem and Twin Falls. Recognizing the importance of parks in the state's developing tourism industry, the Division of Parks and Recreation oversaw the construction of downhill ski slopes at Canaan Valley, of tramways at Pipestem and Hawks Nest and of golf courses at Canaan Valley, Pipestem, Cacapon and Twin Falls. Many parks also developed recreation programs that still facilitate guided nature hikes, children's conservation workshops, mountain music concerts and an array of other activities for guests.

To prevent the park system from overextending the Mountain State's land and financial resources, the 1977 legislature prohibited further expansion of the organization without government approval. Legislators did, however, appropriate funds for improving already existing parks. By the early 1980s new additions included five lodges and a convention center at Canaan Valley, deluxe cottages at North Bend, horseback riding at Pipestem and the restored turn-of-the-century logging town of Cass.

In addition to 37 parks, the West Virginia State Park system also features nine state forests and four wildlife management areas that protect 100,000 acres of West Virginia's wilderness. Regulated by the Department of Parks and Recreation with help from the Division of Forestry, many of the state forests flourish on land once devastated by excessive industrial logging. Unlike the state parks that forbid timber harvesting and hunting on park property, state forests undergo selective timbering and permit in-season hunting.

Under the diligent supervision of the Division of Natural Resources, the Mountain State's parks have evolved into one of America's premier state-run park systems. The parks, forests and wildlife areas offer both the tranquility of untrampled nature and the thrill of sports like skiing and mountain biking. After nearly a century of success, the state parks continue to preserve much of the ecology, splendor and adventure of West Virginia.

An aerial view of Pipestem Resort State Park Lodge in Mercer and Summer counties

A small rainbow highlights the mist below Blackwater Falls, Blackwater Falls State Park in Tucker County.

Watters Smith Memorial State Park in Harrison County preserves pieces of West Virginia's farm history.

*R*ecreation, conservation
and history—the legacy
of the West Virginia State
Park system

Rhododendrons flourish in the dark recesses of Coopers Rock State Forest, east of Morgantown.

Idle rowboats on the lake at Seneca State Forest in Pocahontas County.

Above - Fallen leaves frame a painting-like reflection of fall's final colors in Holly River State Park.

Left - Brilliant traces of autumn come to rest on an old stump.

A lone boater at dawn on Bluestone Lake, Bluestone Lake State Park in Summers County.

Aerial view of Bluestone Lake and dam. Bluestone Dam celebrated 50-years of operation in 1999.

Following pages - A winter storm
envelops Hawks Nest State Park
in Fayette County.

The Blackwater River flows through Blackwater Falls State Park.

The first hints of fall reach the Blackwater Canyon in Blackwater Falls State Park.

The headwaters of the Blackwater River in Canaan Valley State Park

An old family cemetery overlooks the restored pioneer farm in Twin Falls State Park.

Capitol Complex

The massive edifice and monumental gold dome of the West Virginia State Capitol dominate the Charleston skyline with an image of authority. Prior to the building's completion in 1932, the state's seat of government shifted between Wheeling and Charleston three times, occupying five different Capitols in a span of 69 years.

From West Virginia's induction to statehood on June 20, 1863 until the spring of 1870, the Linsly Institute Building in Wheeling served as the first Capitol. However, as early as 1868, legislatures began to discuss resettling the capital in the centrally located city of Charleston. As further enticement, in 1869 the Charleston city council promised to spend $50,000 on public buildings should the state government move south.

On March 28, 1870, the steamboat Mountain Boy departed Wheeling to transport Governor William E. Stevenson, several state officials and numerous government documents to Charleston. The Merchants Bank Building served as a temporary shelter for the transplanted government until the completion of a new Capitol in December 1870.

After only five years, government officials abandoned the new Capitol to return the seat of power to Wheeling. The city of Wheeling built an impressive stone Capitol to welcome back the state government. Nevertheless, unrest over the Capital's location continued until 1877, when the legislature let the citizens of West Virginia decide on a permanent Capitol site. Given the choice of Charleston, Clarksburg or Martinsburg, an overwhelming majority voted for Charleston.

In May 1885, the government once again boarded a steam boat bound for Charleston, earning the nickname the "Floating Capital." A large new, three-story Capitol replaced the original structure on the corner of Capitol and Lee streets. However, on January 3, 1921, fire tore through the edifice, igniting a stockpile of guns and ammunition stored in the attic. The sound of exploding ammunition rang through the valley, as flames razed the capitol.

Following the fire, builders erected a temporary "Pasteboard Capitol" of cheap wood and wallboard that burned to the ground on March 2, 1927. Meanwhile, the legislature appointed the Capitol Building Commission to oversee construction of a permanent Capitol in east Charleston.

The Capitol Building Commission recruited architect Cass Gilbert to draft the new Capitol. Already famous for designing the first skyscraper, several state capitols, and the U.S. Supreme Court and the U.S. Treasury buildings in Washington D.C., Gilbert made the present West Virginia State Capitol his final masterpiece.

Overlooking the Kanawha River, the tremendous building, including east and west wings, central structure and magnificent rotunda, has 333 rooms and a total floor area of 535,000 square feet. Four types of imported and domestic marble comprise much of the interior and a magnificent chandelier made of 10,000 pieces of Czechoslovakian crystal hangs from the apex of the rotunda. The exterior of the Capitol's dome sparkles with a coat of 23.5-carat gold leaf. Other intricacies from carved friezes to elegant columns exemplify the palatial architecture of the Capitol.

In addition to the Capitol, the Capitol Building Commission also appropriated funds for the construction of an executive residence. Architect Walter F. Martens conferred with Gilbert on the design of the Governor's Mansion to ensure harmony between the appearance of the two buildings. Completed in 1925, the stately brick mansion sits adjacent to the Capitol on the corner of Kanawha Boulevard and Greenbrier Street.

Since the Capitol's dedication on June 20, 1932, the Capitol Complex has grown to include several administration buildings and the Cultural Center, home of the West Virginia State Museum, the Division of Culture and History, the Library Commission, the State Archives and History Library and the State Theater. The Cultural Center also features "The Great Hall," a spacious foyer used for receptions, exhibitions and festivals.

Numerous statues and monuments adorn the Capitol grounds, including the West Virginia Veterans Memorial completed in 1995. The circular black granite tribute records the names of West Virginians who perished in World War I, World War II, the Korean War and the Vietnam War. The spacious lawns surrounding the Capitol also host such popular celebrations as Vandalia and the Multi-Cultural Festival.

Boaters enjoy the Kanawha River in front of the state Capitol.

Dancing in the Great Hall of the Cultural Center during the annual
Vandalia Gathering at the Capitol Complex

The magnificent Capitol rotunda

*The stunning permanent home
of the once "Floating Capital"*

Following Pages -
Night settles over the
War Memorial on
the Capitol grounds.

An aerial view of the West Virginia State Capitol Complex and the Kanawha River.

An aerial view of the capital city of Charleston and the Kanawha Valley.

Tamarack

"Passion built this place. Passion fills this place. Passion will make this a West Virginia monument," declared wood worker Michael Ross at the opening of the Tamarack arts and crafts center on June 19, 1996. Located in Beckley, Tamarack markets more than 10,000 *West Virginia-Made* products, and features a gourmet cafe, theater, art galleries, studios, gardens and more. One of the 1,800 juried West Virginia artisans, authors and specialty food producers whose wares fill the stunning showcase, Ross captured in his words the pride and emotion that run through the Mountain State's long craft tradition.

Named after the deciduous tamarack tree that, like Mountaineers, has a reputation for strength and perseverance, Tamarack celebrates the artistry and heritage of West Virginia. The circular building's scarlet peaks give Tamarack the appearance not only of the top of a tamarack tree, but also of a star quilt pattern or the mountains at sunset. Inside, the airy facility reflects a graceful blend of down-home character and sophistication. Blown glass figurines rest on hand carved wooden tables flanked by pottery vessels, iron sculptures and reed baskets. Beeswax candles, jewelry, wreaths and intricate stained glass pieces form elegant clusters along with a myriad of other masterpieces. In addition, a special section features books, cassettes and videos by West Virginia authors and performing artists. Tamarack selects each of their contributing artisans through a jury process that ensures the center promotes, as its motto suggests, *The Best of West Virginia.*

From quilts to cane chairs, dulcimers to dancing jacks, much of Tamarack's merchandise represents craftsmanship practiced in the hills of Appalachia since the arrival of European settlers in the 1700s. Tamarack's shelves of *West Virginia-Made* food products brim with such old-time favorites as wilted lettuce salad dressing, strawberry-rhubarb jam and apple butter. The "A Taste of West Virginia" eatery in Tamarack offers traditional Appalachian fare like fried green tomato sandwiches and country fried potatoes. Under management of The Greenbrier Resort, the cafe also serves more epicurean entrees made from indigenous ingredients including fresh vegetables marinated in ramp vinaigrette and pan-fried West Virginia rainbow trout.

Five glass-walled studios allow Tamarack shoppers to observe resident and visiting artists at work. The facility also schedules craft demonstrations, workshops and festivals, as well as screens historical films and hosts performing arts groups from around the state. Herb, botanical and sculpture gardens, nature trails, an outdoor eating area and a playground stocked with hand-crafted toys make the grounds surrounding Tamarack fun for folks of all ages.

The Tamarack center grew out of former Governor Gaston Caperton's desire to provide West Virginia artisans with a year-round, in-state market for their handiwork. Under his guidance, the West Virginia Parkways Authority first began stocking travel plazas with *West Virginia-Made* retail items. The rapid success of the road-side craft-shops inspired the establishment of a singular arts and crafts showcase. With input from representatives, artisans, community leaders and others from all 55 West Virginia counties, Tamarack, from concept to construction, became the collective work of West Virginians. Clint Bryan and Associates of Charleston designed the edifice, and today the organization still employs only state residents.

The nation's first state-run craft center and one of the Mountain State's premier tourist stops, Tamarack offers more than 500,000 visitors per year *The Best of West Virginia.*

Early morning sun strikes Tamarack, West Virginia's premier arts and crafts center.

Members of Les Dynamics Choir learn about Emerald Stained Glass from Pam Bell.

A potter absorbed in her art.

The skilled hands of a basket weaver

"The Best of West Virginia"

Aerial view of Tamarack near Beckley

Skies clear over Tamarack after the 1998 blizzard.

Following Pages - The sun rises over
the headwaters of the Kanawha
River formed by the confluence of
the Gauley River and New River at
Gauley Bridge in Fayette County.

National Radio Astronomy Observatory

In the stillness of the Deer Creek Valley, against a quiet landscape of rolling farmland and surrounding mountains, protrude the steel dishes of several radio telescopes. Powerful implements of the National Radio Astronomy Observatory (NRAO), the electro-sensitive telescopes draw scientists from around the world to study the mysteries of the universe. The first national radio observatory constructed in the United States, the facility in Green Bank, Pocahontas County, remains one of only three such research stations in the country.

Through the interception and interpretation of electromagnetic waves emanating from stars, supernovas, galaxies, quasars and pulsars, radio astronomers map the objects' images, properties and relative ages. Because every substance, like hydrogen or ammonia, emits energy at a specific frequency, scientists can ascertain the components of various cosmic entities. Receiving electromagnetic waves from objects millions of light years away, meaning waves millions of years old, helps researchers determine the age of objects and hypothesize about the universe's evolutionary time scale. As approximately 90 percent of the heavens remain imperceptible with optical tele-scopes, the discovery of radio astronomy in the mid-twentieth century has inspired new theories on the origin and development of the universe.

In the early 1930s, when Bell Laboratories engineer Karl Jansky set up an experiment to determine static sources that might distort reception on the transatlantic telephone line, he did not expect to hear from the Milky Way. Nor did he intend to spawn a scientific discipline focused on the farthest reaches of the universe. Jansky first picked up the celestial signal with a movable, aerial antenna he constructed in a New Jersey field. Rotating the device, he received several radio waves. Two came from thunderstorms, the third the Milky Way.

Following World War II, astronomers began taking an active interest in Jansky's results. In 1954, realizing the immensity and expense of the equip-ment needed to further radio astronomy, an assembly of scientists petitioned the National Science Foundation (NSF) for funds to construct a national radio astronomy research station. The NSF allocated the money and named a nonprofit organization of nine prestigious universities, known as Associated Universities Inc. to supervise construction and operation of the National Radio Astronomy Observatory. The astronomers decided to locate the new research center at Green Bank due to the area's lack of electrical activity and industry that might disturb the accuracy of electro-sensitive instruments.

By 1988, the NRAO at Green Bank had grown to include eight telescopes of varying sizes when the observatory's most heavily used 300-foot telescope collapsed from metal fatigue. The crash fueled a 95 million dollar project to build the "world's largest fully steerable radio telescope."

Scientists and engineers at the NRAO began working with engineers from Radiation Systems Inc. to design a durable, highly sensitive, super telescope. Complete after almost 10 years of construction, the new state-of-the-art structure, named the Green Bank Telescope (GBT), at 485-feet tall surpasses the Statue of Liberty in height and weighs 16 million pounds.

More than 200,000 scientists each year compete in a stringent application process that admits approximately 250 researchers access to Green Bank telescopes. Dormitories on the observatory premises and an extensive support staff accommo-date the visiting astronomers as they listen to the heavens.

The pinnacle of radio astronomy technology, the Green Bank Telescope towers above the pastoral countryside surrounding the National Radio Astronomy Observatory.

When finished, the Green Bank Telescope will operate as the largest fully steerable radio telescope in the world.

The Reber Telescope—the world's first parabolic radio telescope.

Completed in 1965, the 140-Foot Telescope holds the record as the largest equatorially-mounted telescope in use.

The 20-Meter Telescope determines highly accurate time, in addition to measuring the earth's motion.

$$R_c = c\,\tau_0\,\Omega_0\,\left|1 + q_0 - 3\Omega_0/2\right|^{-3/2}$$

(Scalesize of the Universe)

Above - The sun slips behind a hill at the Green Bank observatory, leaving clouds ablaze in dramatic evening tones.

Right - A moody sky rumbles over Green Bank's 140-Foot Telescope.

Following Page - The sun rises over the confluence of the Potomac and Shenandoah rivers at Harpers Ferry.

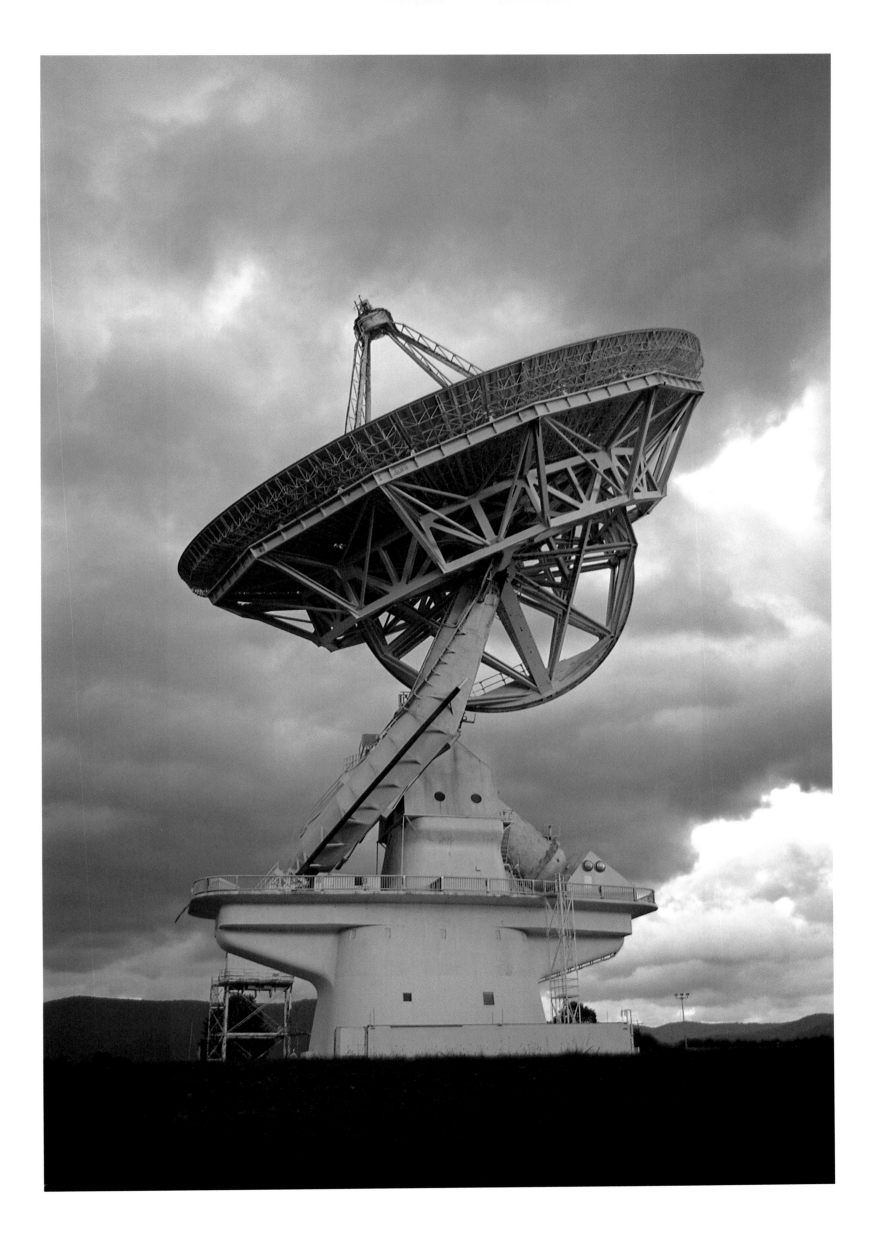

Spring

Each spring the famous gardens at
Oglebay Park in Wheeling burst
into an extravagant display of tulips.
These tulips closed on a freezing
April morning.

Summer

Above - Anthony Creek in Greenbrier County reflects a tranquil summer afternoon.

Right - A field of wildflowers in late summer, near Green Bank.

Fall

Autumn in the hills of Jackson County

Winter

Above - Aerial view of Stephens Lake in Raleigh County, following a blizzard. The lake offers more than 15-miles of shoreline for fishing and camping.

Right - Snow lends a magical aura to a stand of pine trees in Tucker County.

The People of West Virginia

Like the varied cloth of a quilt, the people of West Virginia represent a patchwork of human history sewn together by the land they call home. Names such as Kanawha, Seneca and Mingo, burial mounds, artifacts and a few scattered descendants remain of the many Native American tribes that once roamed the area. The spirited perseverance of the region's early European settlers still thrives in the hills and hollows that now support a population of diverse ethnicities. Whether African-American or Irish, Filipino or Hungarian, the people of the Mountain State share a special land. The colloquialism, "once a West Virginian, always a West Virginian," seems to recognize some transcendent magic of the mountains that continues to echo in the hearts and minds of all who leave.

While land speculators and fur trappers made the first Caucasian forays into present-day West Virginia, groups of German, Scotch-Irish and British settlers followed in the early 1700s. Fleeing religious oppression in their homeland, German pacifists began arriving in the fertile lowlands of Pennsylvania as early as 1650. As the number of refugees outgrew the availability of farmland, immigrants followed Native American trails into the foreboding wilderness of the Allegheny Mountains. Braving dense forests, harsh weather and the threat of Native American attacks, in the late 1720s the Germans succeeded in establishing the town of "Mecklenburg," now Shepherdstown, in contemporary Jefferson County. German immigrants continued to spread west along the South Branch of the Potomac River forming settlements such as Harman, Hinkle, Kile, German Valley and Dolly (Dahle) Sods.

Like the Germans, Scotch-Irish families escaped political unrest in northern Ireland by sailing to the "New World." Following the same footpaths that led German settlers into the Alleghenies, the Scotch-Irish nestled deep in the hollows of the ancient hills. British pioneers also risked the untamed interior of western Virginia, settling in the South Branch Valley, throughout the Allegheny highlands and in the Ohio and Kanawha valleys. More than a century later, in 1869, a knot of Swiss immigrants found the landscape of Randolph County so reminiscent of Switzerland that they established a community bearing the nation's Latin name, Helvetia.

Throughout the latter half of the 19th-century, West Virginia swelled with people seeking employment in the fledgling state's booming industries. Although a small number of African-Americans had labored in the salt works of the Kanawha Valley since the 1830s, the end of the Civil War inspired an influx of freed slaves into the state, first as track laying crews with the railroads, and then as miners and lumberjacks. In the 1880s, coal companies recruited, sometimes directly from Ellis Island, Hungarian, Polish, Romanian, Russian and other eastern European immigrants to work in West Virginia mines. The companies also imported Italian stone masons to lay retaining walls, mine entrances and bridge trestles in the late 1890s. Walls and bridges around the state still bear the craftsmanship of Italian masters. In addition, the coalfields drew Jewish merchants from Philadelphia and New Jersey to manage company stores and other local businesses.

The arrival of Greeks, Indians and Asians further diversified the Mountain State's populace. Following World War I, a number of Greek refugees left ravaged homes in Europe for Virginia, eventually migrating into southern West Virginia. Predominately joining the medical community as doctors and nurses, Indians and people of various Asian ethnicities, including Thai, Filipino and Vietnamese settled in the state after 1960.

The many heritages of West Virginia's citizenry survive as colorful strands woven into a tapestry of mountain culture. The handicrafts, holiday customs, music and even dialect of the state's early settlers flourish today in the creations of craft artisans, musicians and in the continued use of such words as "ain't" and "afeared." The Italian Heritage Festival in Clarksburg, the African American Jubilee in Wheeling and the Ocktoberfest in Shepherdstown, all celebrate ethnic traditions present in the Mountain State. At the outset of a new millennium, West Virginia continues to thrive as a place blessed by both the land and its people.

Kelly Allen, as a child growing up in Charleston, nuzzles a puppy amid wind-blown red buds.

Montani Semper Liberi
Mountaineers Are Always Free

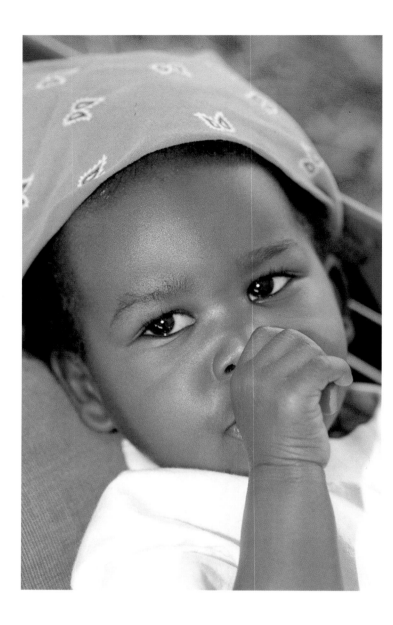

Left - One-and-a-half-year old Hannah Williams lounges in a red wagon at the annual Mountain State Arts and Crafts Fair in Ripley.

Below - With bright eyes and a dashing smile, James Domonique Keys of Lewisburg embodies the playful spirit of childhood summers.

Descended from predominately Irish ancestors, Mary Hamm and her late husband Harry raised their 12 children in Wheeling. With the patient smile and compassionate eyes of a dedicated mother, Mary sits surrounded by photographs of her family.

Left - Long a resident of Coalwood, 81-year old "Red" Carroll's face reflects the character and dignity of a lifetime spent in the hills of West Virginia. Red has gained recent fame for appearing as a character in Homer Hickam, Jr.'s memoirs, The *Rocket Boys.* Made into the major motion picture, *October Sky*, the heart-warming, true story features Red's son, Jimmy O'Dell, as one of the "Rocket Boys."

Below - Beckley resident Donna Cernuto sits among hand-crafted art pieces at Tamarack. As a Tamarack employee, she welcomes guests with her lively smile.

After 17 years as an underground miner, Ronald S. Greer now guides visitors through the Beckley Exhibition Coal Mine. His tour includes information on mining history and technology, mine tales and home-spun humor.

The Ross sisters of Wallace have all distinguished themselves in the arts; Ellen as an award-winning pianist (above-left), Lydia a budding dancer and actress (above) and Hannah as a gifted fiddler well-known throughout West Virginia (left). All three also perform in a family band called the Ebenezer Stringband.

Taken 30 years ago, the above photograph captures a very special pair of sisters. Leora and Lynn Tusing lived and worked their entire lives on a farm that their grandfather settled in 1866 atop Branch Mountain. Even as elderly women, the Mennonite sisters continued to farm, hunt and secure an income weaving and selling wool and linen coverlets.

Acknowledgments

I owe the deepest affection and gratitude to my daughter, Lucia, with whom I shared the creation of this book, and to my wonderful wife Teresa, who has traveled many miles with me in search of photographic opportunities. I am grateful for her patience, wisdom and great company. I wish to thank my parents who have always been supportive and a source of inspiration. I also want to recognize professional geologist Amy Whitaker for writing the technical piece on West Virginia's geology. Amy is a graduate of West Virginia University. Fellow photographers Stephen J. Shaluta Jr. and David Fattaleh offered assistance and advice on such difficult lighting situations as illuminating a coal mine and a railroad steam engine. Bill Archer and Dr. Ray Swick gave suggestions, research material and proofreading time to specific text pieces in their fields of expertise. Harry Price, Caryn Gresham and Hoy Murphy also spent time proofreading the copy. I would like to give special acknowledgment to our graphic artist, Denise Dodson, for her time and artistry. I also have had the honor to be associated with the fine people at the Division of Natural Resources for numerous years. While working with this excellent state agency I learned many of the skills necessary to assemble a book such as *West Virginia: The Land and its People.*

As West Virginians, we continue to thrive in a direct and delicate relationship with the land that beckons us to respect and care for the piece of earth that we call home, for the land that sustained our ancestors and will greet our children.